If It Comes to That

If It Comes to That

Poems by

Marc Frazier

Cover design by Shay Culligan
Cover art painted by Steven Ostrowski

ISBN: 978-1-63980-424-5

Kelsay Books
502 South 1040 East, A-119
American Fork, Utah 84003
Kelsaybooks.com

A God you understood would be less than yourself.
—Flannery O'Connor

Acknowledgments

Thank you to the following publications, where versions of these poems previously appeared, sometimes with different titles:

Ariel Chart: "The Visit"
As it Ought to Be Magazine: "Sent My Way"
Bird's Thumb: "If It Comes to That"
BlazeVox16: "Kahlo"
Bloom: "Wild Reeds"
Caveat Lector and *Finishing Line Press:* "Higher Love"
Cypress Journal: "On Any Given Day You Are"
Eastern Iowa Review: "Waiting to Grow Up"
Euonia Review: "Cape Cod Evening," "What a Difference a Day"
Free State Review: "Silent Movie"
Gargoyle: "Design," "Journal of the Plague Years: One"
Ginosko Literary Journal: "Sometimes a Bunny Is Only . . .," "Indochine," "What to Do with Entirely," "Cape Cod Evening," "What a Difference a Day"
Global Poemic: "The Rite of Spring"
Gloom Cupboard: "The Maiden with the Rose on Her Forehead"
Guesthouse: "Black Box"
Hole in the Head Review: "A Month in the Country"
Last Leaves: "The Scent of the Sea"
The Laurel Review: "The Blind Leading the Blind"
Limp Wrist: "While Birds Sing: A Villanelle"
Lothlorien Poetry Journal: "Shifting," "What Does It Take to Be Happy"
The MacGuffin: "Desire"
The McNeese Review: "Now"
The Miscreant: "Mother of IRA Leader Tries to Bury Her Son"
NatureWriting: "Disciple"
New World Writing: "Journal of the Plague Years: Two," "Women in Movies"
Nixes Mate: "Three Fridas"

Olentangy Review: "Miss Willoughby"
The Outrider Review: "White Rooms"
Passager: Pandemic Diaries: "It Has Come to That"
Poetry Bay: "Rivera"
Praxis: "Vigil"
River and South Review: "Incident on the Green Line"
Rust + Moth: "A Painted Lady Can Be a House or a Butterfly"
The Rye Whiskey Review: "One Life," "Lauderdale," "On Any Given Day You Are"
Sledgehammer: "Nova Scotia"
South 85 Journal: "A Pound of American Flesh" (under title "Fallujah 2004")
South Shore Review: "Gathering"
Spectrum: The Identity Zine: "The Defiant Morning"
Split Rock Review: "After"
Stone Poetry Journal: "Realms: Demeter and Persephone"
Sublunary Review: "I'm Afraid by Then He Was Only Sad"
The Tampa Review: "All About Us"
Unlikely Stories: "Nocturne on the North Shore"
West Trade Review: online exclusive, "All Evening the Luna Moths"
Whale Road Review: "Choosing Pumpkins"
Woolgathering: "Marked"
Writers Block Magazine: "The Lover of Horses," "Knowledge"

Anthologies

Collateral Damage: "Human Declaration for the Return of the Children," "Bulletproof Blanket for Kids"

Credits

Line of poetry quoted in "Choosing Pumpkins" is from Richard Siken's book *Crush.*

Phrase "ship was built to wreck," in "I'm Afraid by Then He Was Only Sad" references the song by Florence and the Machine.

"Even the trees know it." Line by Anne Sexton.

Italicized phrases and lines in poem *Indochine* are dialogue from movie *Indochine.*

Italicized lines in "Disciple" are from Mary Oliver.

Title "The Centre Cannot Hold" is from poem "The Second Coming" by William Butler Yeats.

Contents

All About Us

NOAA Fisheries Pacific Islands' dolphin viewing guidelines threaten a large tourist industry, especially in Hawaii.
—www.fpir.noaa.gov/PRD/prd_swim_with_wild_dolphins.html—

We are tired of us
the constant glare
of screens
with conflicting data

brain patterns fracture
attention spans shrink

The dolphins are tired of us
our need to be soothed
swarms of us who
invade their pods

throw off their
echolocation
their speech to one another

they want rest after feeding all night

their sleep cycles disrupted
they swim to places
where predators wait

but what delight to see them break water
and spin
such joy

starved for
the spiritual
our need for play
staying fifty feet away
is a tease

when we leave
everything everywhere
will be with us again
as we aim to integrate split
screens split lives

Now

—All the new thinking is about loss.
In this it resembles all the old thinking . . .
—Robert Hass

You put ax to wood with angry thrusts:
an arsonist without something to burn.
If only we knew how to manage what we have:
that impatience waiting for water to boil.
Why can't we just sit out front toothless
and drink moonshine from jars
and be happy for once?
Why can't we use apologies with the rattler removed?

A fabulist run out of tales is the new version of us.
The old version crackled with exquisite detail:
emerald, brocade, blue flame, comet.
We need tinder for a slow taking off—
none of the crackling abandon of skin burning fire,
my tongue on your sweaty nipples an epilogue
after all the most important words have been used.

Are we without light: *black stones, black clouds?*
These are things I still marvel at:
How marble and immortality go together in an artist's eye
How medievalists believed in the signature of all things—
God's imprint on every natural object
Birthing mares relieving their newborns hooves first
The flow of tango steps that appear unpracticed
Balm of crushed leaves and herbs on wounds.
Hummingbird, harbor, groundwater, dune.

Marked

Like Moses for greatness. Like *Juden* for a Jewish shop owner. The gold star in a family's window to honor the sacrifice of their brave son. Sheep or goat's blood smeared above doors in the Old Testament so the Angel of Death passed by. The large "X" on the diseased elms of my youth. I remember standing by our tree destined to be destroyed. I, too, wanted to disappear. I leaned against its doomed bark listening to the sound of a bird's lonely warbling. I, too wanted to sing. Now every time I hear this bird trill, I feel abandoned and alone. I think about an origami bird I once saw unfolding and unfolding to reveal the creases that made the bird disappear. A psychic told me I was "one of the watched ones." Was it by one of the guardian angels the nuns spoke of? I wanted to believe they would not mark our house, or believe they would, for what went on in it, like paint sploshed on doors where someone has the plague.

Kahlo

A body tortured, womb misshapen, impaled—
the violent crash heard in all her work.

In the beginning mirrors reshape
her as she lies unable to see

what she needs to, a life
to follow: a coded, surreal art.

The body, the psyche processing trauma—
attempts at childbirth futile.

How many ways can a body betray?
How many ways can a man?

Lust and passion, the need for him again.
What if she cuts her hair, wears his suit?

Who is she
as scissors in her hand menace?

Do we want her to exhaust her suffering?
Who is who they wanted to become?

Rivera

There: the infant in the bulb of a plant
warmed by earth: a life born to flower.

Oversized women nestle lilies, anything:
the cradle of their fleshy arms a womb.

A man's privilege:
the macho gesture of posing mistresses for posterity.

How much he bends to his will
as he takes the gringo dollar: bold claims:

indigenous and communal man:
stock images on public spaces.

In the end a self-portrait of time's wasting
an old man's face: cliché on canvas.

For whom does the artist speak?
Who is who they claim to be?

Nova Scotia

The only museum worth seeing
is the Maritime Museum in Halifax.
There is nothing false or practiced about anything in it
and they don't have a gift shop.
They have pieces of ships (such as a figurehead or cannon),

items associated with shipping like
uniforms with buttons that really make a statement.
I sat through the video in the small dark room
three times because I could and no one would ask why
or tell me to move on, you've looked at this painting long enough.

The most famous museums are the worst.
Just monuments to empire showing off how much that culture
    accumulated
no matter who they stole from.
The "Masters," people say as if we should all
genuflect and make the sign of the cross.

The Maritime Museum is real and when you walk back
onto the streets of Halifax that all lead
down to the sea tasting the salty air
you know sailors love their lives,
and the loneliness inside you is deeper than the sea.

After

Cadmium in the Earth's crust—the bluish grey of the manor house they built after the new hatreds arrived, but before the purge. Its floorboards creak-proof, the soil of its grounds perfect compost for red rhododendron, white hydrangea. A nest of new ideas pulse. I focus on any single star as if it will stir nostalgia for another time, a time unfelt at other times. Instead, a chasm opens, consumes any passion I have left. Rampant emotion disallowed. Joy deceased. Put in boxes for the attic. The acquisition of sense paramount. I hold crystals for protection, flee to the ocean, its reefs, my sense of self distorted by what feels like my last desperate gasp. A canopy of sky blurs through waves of water. My limbs nearly fail me as if I were suddenly elderly, my skin parchment and tearable by coral. I feel a sparrow flutter in my heart as I recall our last luxuriant moments when language unraveled like DNA between us. The forest of pines, fields of lavender a shared memory, rusty and filtered through hazy light. Now I dream of suffering, decay, a thread of semen, that longing assailed by aftershocks of violence. Aphids in the still breathing tulips I gather in my arms. They are the flesh I desire, the moment that does not pass. I am an empire of cells, I think, a hoard of blood waiting to be spilled.

Human Declaration for the Return of the Children

—from blind translation of Marjorie Agosin's poem:
"Declaración humana par los derechos del niño"

We all know the children
who have disappeared to mirror the earth
a vineyard of violet color
o like a ray of joy
the sky their best-loved turtle
upside down

We all know children who have disappeared
with the sway of the moon
with the weight of a canopy of green guavas
We all know the children
who have disappeared from milk
from chocolate to abandon their aunts

We all know the children who are gone
from the memory of corn
from the tempo of their cradles
dancers who descend and bend
We all know the children
who have disappeared
from their books the furry bears
that held them the alphabet from love
to the silence of the authorities

We all know the children
who have disappeared
from peace and left to war
gathered innocents
each alone a flawless gem
a hand that gives and not takes
We all know the children
hidden jewels blooming stars
fast dancing through pathways to the sky

The Maiden with the Rose on Her Forehead

We are always at the dump. Men shoot rats. I don't feel threatened. It seems a natural part of the male world in which my father and I live. He looks for parts while I wander aimlessly through the rubble spilling its guts. Flies are everywhere. I wonder at some of the items I see lying about, at how people choose what to discard, what to hold on to. My father and I live in a lean-to by the Kishwaukee, a river swarming with carp. One day a microburst blows through and our home is gone. We spend a great deal of time looking for materials to build a new life. I want something better than the old one, but it doesn't seem to be shaping up that way—the same blankets and tarps attach to trees to hunker down under, a firepit, fetid mattresses covered with clothes on which to sleep. I find an old tintype among the refuse. It has the design of a young woman with the pattern of a rose on her forehead. I set her beside my mattress on top of a wobbly stand. I recall the Madonna from the old days of going to church. I call her Mary and dream at night beside her with the river flowing through me.

Cape Cod Evening

—Edward Hopper

I enter this evening to join them.
The dog, alert to the song of a whippoorwill,
still in the strange, long, blonde grass
extending into a stand of pines.
The grass rubs my shins and calves
as I greet the animated collie who twirls around twice
and stretches out its front legs in downward dog.
I pet it vigorously speaking with assurance.
Behind us rises a solid house—
window shades perfectly aligned, white lace curtains still.
A man in a white tee shirt sits on the one-step stoop,
and off to his side stands a stiff, thick-set, blonde woman,
arms crossed in tenseness shutting out
the evening sounds, their pet, the man close by.
She will stand there, I realize, as grass grows up her green dress.
The man stares down at something I can't make out.
I say hello to both and get no response,
saunter to join the strange, blue pines alive with birdsong.

What a Difference a Day

The one who got away returns at times amid the routine because today is not enough. It has to be enough or why go on? Sometimes I think of the one day of Mrs. Dalloway's story. The worry over the flowers, her thoughts flowing like converging rivers. The quotidian is the backbone of any tale. Any day. That's why the element of surprise is so necessary. That's why an orchestra of thunderstorms matters. My rituals vary little. I try to be mindful and make any task about being present in the here and now. Washing dishes can be a form of meditation. But it is not so easy to trudge along against the current of the ordinary, the expected. Daydreams are real and let me wander anonymous fields or hear the waterfall we walked three miles to see. I try to believe I'm better than laundry day self. Wasn't string theory supposed to explain all this? Where is the furious ecstasy, the dance of the dervish, the tune I can fit in my pocket? Where is the avalanche of affection I was expecting? Instead, there is cleaning the cat's water bowl, recycling, signing in at the doctor's. A novel's gathering storm can be more real to me than the daily frequency I tune to: the day stuck on one playlist like the long talks of lovers that lead everywhere but nowhere, turn back in on themselves and arrive where they began. Life is a plot line with a single resolution, and we are reborn again and again.

While Birds Sing: A Villanelle

I want to say I'll never go away.
Sometimes I wish a season will end.
You arrive full of need every day.

We both need to keep fear at bay.
Our words break but never seem to bend.
I want to say I'll never go away.

When dawn comes, I'll know what to say.
Imagine a letter I don't intend to send.
You arrive full of need every day.

While lilacs last, I ask you to stay.
Summer's end tames my desperation to tend.
I want to say I'll never go away.

At times the moon's waxing prompts me to pray.
Strong joining can untie like a fisherman's bend.
You arrive full of need every day.

We can't predict how much our grief will weigh.
Or why our choices cause a wall to ascend.
I want to say I'll never go away.
You arrive full of need every day.

Swayed by Love

You think you have agreed to this,
what has been done with your life, willingly.
—Tess Gallagher

-1-

In Halifax, streets lead down to the harbor
where ghosts of mariners greet me.
I walk streets Adele Hugo walked—
cobbled together with her obsession
(can it be called love?) for her lieutenant.
I weep and no one notices.
Collapse each night.
My one prayer—to begin to live.

I drive through wilderness to the Bay of Fundy's heavy clouds,
moss on boulders that nest like giant eggs beside the dock.
What remains is vast/unseeable.

On to Peggy's Cove.
Like loaves and fish, this village swells to a million visitors
snapping photos—
 the requisite lighthouse perched on sea-swept rocks,
 fishing boats moored to docks, lobster traps stacked beside
 the inlet, modest houses dotting hills.

A poetic vision anywhere I turn: a black-clothed figure
on layered rock slabs against a blue sky.
How much life can I hold in my head?
How much should I tip for this tragic tale
 of Peggy, storm-tossed maiden,
 for this salty
 air, the wind?

-2-

In French films, love-obsessed women collapse in foreign sands—
the blank stare of the self-abandoned.
What strength or weakness it takes to forget one's self.

Lili spends her days sketching an absent lover in coves/cafes.
I'd like to open myself fully to another—a forever-open border.
There are always islands to run to like Lili did—
self-absorbed lands of perimeter.
How to guard on so many fronts?
For a while it's a holiday, a spree—
all those sea resorts—water & diamonds.
Spending the stolen wealthy capitalists' money.

And me with my Bartleby existence counting minutes & dollars.
What if artists like Lili had taken today's psychotropics?
Can great art be culled from the easy pill?

-3-

Today I want to give my students chocolate & send them away.
To take soundings of my humanity/
To measure the depth of my regret/Can it be quantified?

I want like a child—that dazzling, temporary thing.
Living wraps me in layers of geologic time—
at times flotsam, other times, something with a root.

I wait for a body to match mine for a moment.
Before summer lengthens beyond memory.
Beyond a body's ability to matter.

The sound of waves stills me as I was calmed after Communion.
A yellow finch basks in the pine's shadow.
His heart beats warmly in the light & in the dark.

It is time to let go of summer—a golden seam between seasons.
Each day will matter more.
            Or less.

Without clichés my life would deepen and mean.
Fetch a better price.
But I distance. Hesitate at shoreline.
Listen most to those who say the least.

-4-

I've not forgotten the long skirts that made you beautiful
in any light/the wandering Jews/coleus we nurtured
in ten-cent pots in rented rooms/
autumn in Shawnee Forest/a confidence you shared.
I hear it in the wind tonight—past and present—
twin versions of what I carry

Eating something spicy, bitter, and sweet at Maya del Sol
            to wake my heart
            as bees confer about summer's end
            as bright blossoms take stock of their dwindling options,
            as the bold birds of Florida choose their next lives.

Higher Love

1.

Ice lights the dark pines.
Beauty of red wings in flight.

The soul its own silent shelter.
Each conscious thing devoted to the single thought of Psyche.

Her altar—the sun, stars.
Venus's, the goddess of love, is cold ash.

Enter Apollo.
Weary of *Who is the fairest?*

His set: rocky hill, sheer precipice of intervention,
wind to carry her, choiceless, to a sunny meadow.

*

How love—knowing only the shape of Cupid's ardor—
heft of shoulder, span of brow?

All husbands: mysteries.

She must know him to know herself.

*

So sudden—the shining wave of Beauty.
The light of *him* dwarfs the light she carries.

Knowledge does not tie one to another.
Trust flees: an injured god.

2.

Begin—the trials.
Venus vows to break her spirit, the will to love,
to ensure her dying with the sparrow,
the sunflower, the silent moss.

Golden fleece catches in her fingers.
A sip of tide from the River Styx.

Venus: Can it be one's nature is not fixed?
Each god is a will, surely.

The final test: her journey below.
Psyche opens the box, not knowing, even now, her place.

*

Love is more than desire.
She awakens to an arrow's prick,

but he captures more than this.

Jove's nectar warms her into godhead.

Now—not the same thought that made her.

The Visit

You slip through the maze of my life softly as ashes
Smell my freshly ground Lavazza

Sit across from me always early to each day's party/
Getting my mail, I imagine a card from you

Mixed in with catalogs and pleas for money
Words of encouragement like you used to send

Buoying me up to help avert another crash/
I walk through my neighborhood rife with impatiens, hostas,

Lilies of the valley, know you are deadheading the pink petunias/
I spot a cardinal and know it is you come to join me

This sign of God whose chirps I recognize as your affectionate
    words/
Evening brings you in your slippers

A wraith in a loose nightdress attune to the evening song
The day a drink empty but for shadows/

Your wishes for me sprawled in perfect
Penmanship upon the patient night

Pasture of Dead Horses

—title from a phrase in a Donald Hall poem

As a child there was a single horse in a field that would come to the fence to greet us. Someone told us to bring sugar cubes for it so we did—geometric gifts the horse nuzzled from our palms. I never wondered where this horse came from or why there was only one of him or if he served any purpose. I was a child and lived by my senses. I petted the long, graceful slope from his forelock to his muzzle and marveled at the placement of his eyes. If I could have said the word beauty that is what I would have named him. If I had more words then I would have asked what was going to happen to him. I understood the word pasture but not the word dead.

Gathering

I carry memories into fields of wildflowers.
Will they ever die
or will reminders forever be torn
from our basements, attics, crowded closets?
Sweet slumber, Sea sedge, Sweet anise.

So rare to gather with siblings,
it would be nice to not always
speak of the deceased,
look at mother's seventh-grade autograph book
dredged from its hiding place.
Lillium, Lonicera, French willow herb.

To not carry the dead with me on prairie paths.
But so much reminds me of them.
Orange root, Oxalis, Oswego tea.

Sitting on the fenced-in patio
we sip iced tea, forage through a box
of mementos, me thinking
we'd gone through this already.
Rock lily, Rosa, Rue anemone.

Will they ever die?
So many sentences lead to a memoriam.
Spring orchis, Trillium, Trumpet ash.

Walks with these flowers relieve some of the weight.
How much time is left in which to matter?
Birthroot, Angelica, Love knot.

Ode as a Grecian Urn

—with phrases from Keat's poem

The Poet's Unearthing

His lyric: ancient scenes on a plundered urn.
The public will adore his claim that unheard melodies

Are sweeter. O arrogant poet! Slave to Empire!
To condescend to them as simple rural folk

Announce their streets for evermore will silent be
Because you picture an idyllic village emptied.

You'd rather have a silent form with marble men
And maidens, a mysterious priest for a hint of the pagan.

Poetry as a testament to that which lasts: an ode or
Objects behind glass in a museum to dominion.

Villagers Uncaptured by the Sculptor

Others are hidden like me. Once our neighbors leave
In mad pursuit to be seized for the artist's urn,

We celebrate the day; a brazen orgy, that's what this living
Is: No lovers are left forever panting like the poet says.

For we are not trapped on a Sylvan historian's artifact.
Though we know we must fade, our melodies echo

To the sensual ear, sweeter than imagined ones.
The sculptor's creation is a human urge.

To be captured once is art,
To be crated off to England, theft.

Those captured on an urn will never return,
But we are here loudly making merry,

Joyous not to be stopped for eternity.
Not a Cold Pastoral but friends to man chanting:

"Living is passion, passion life.
Life's to be lived not frozen in time."

Saving

—using all the words from the poem "This Is Just to Say"
by William Carlos Williams

In the icebox
The plums that were
I have eaten

So sweet for breakfast
And which were
Delicious to you

And they were so cold
forgive me
Say this is probably just

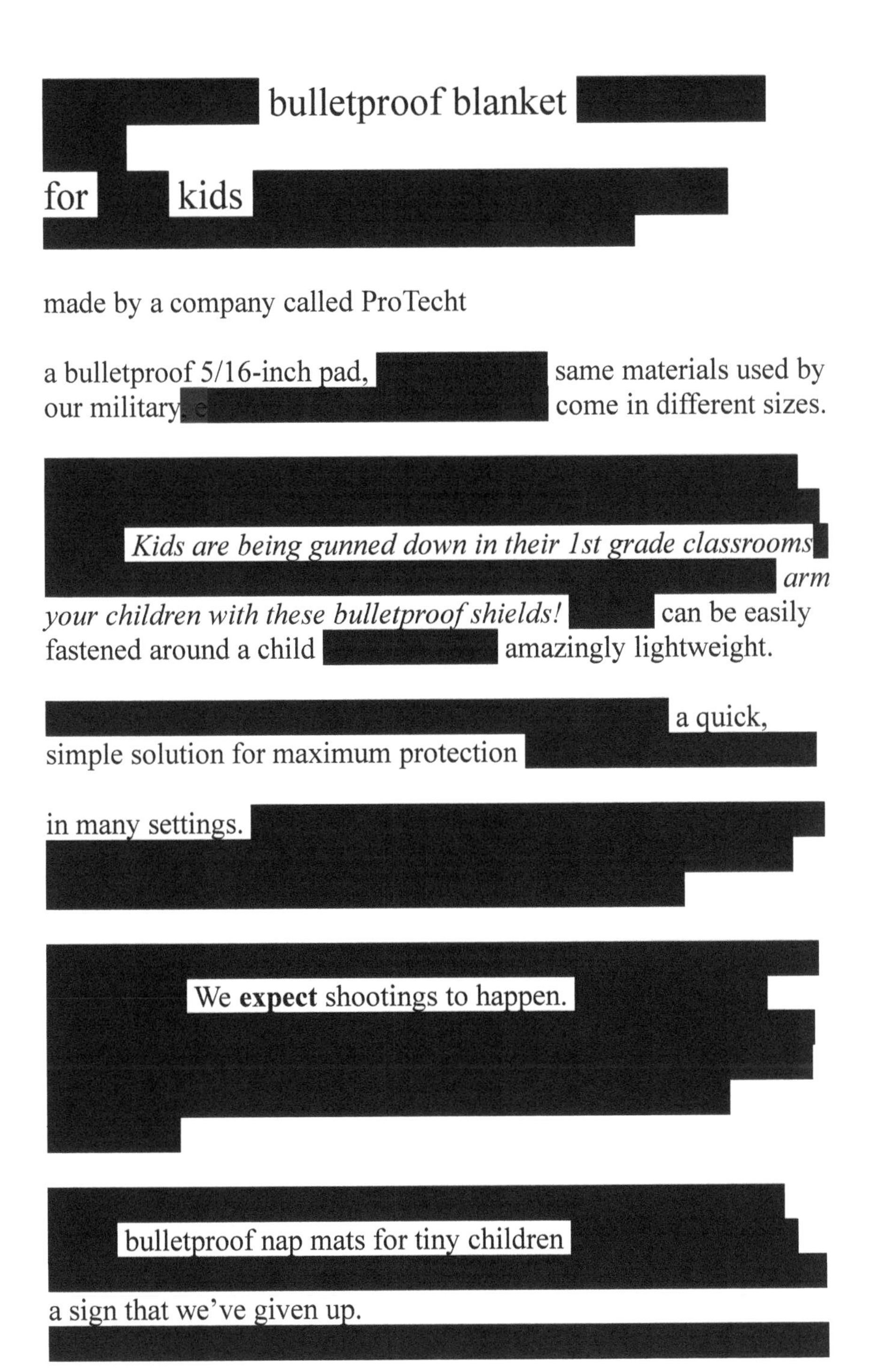

bulletproof blanket

for kids

made by a company called ProTecht

a bulletproof 5/16-inch pad, same materials used by our military come in different sizes.

Kids are being gunned down in their 1st grade classrooms arm your children with these bulletproof shields! can be easily fastened around a child amazingly lightweight.

a quick, simple solution for maximum protection

in many settings.

We **expect** shootings to happen.

bulletproof nap mats for tiny children

a sign that we've given up.

The Discovery

What does it mean? Finding a fetus along the Kishwaukee River bank. News gets around fast, the school abuzz. How are we supposed to react when we hear? I picture the boys who found it already imagining their new notoriety when they tell this tale. I could have been one of them out with my fellow Boy Scouts. What would we have done when we figured out what it was? This was way before cell phones. We needed to tell our parents. Is this some kind of crime? An accident? Did it involve one of our classmates? Do our teachers seem changed somehow by the knowledge of it? Are they uncomfortable that we know about it? Adults confident and full of judgment might whisper about this because they don't want to think we are capable of creating life. Or destroying it. We forget quickly, titillated by its shock value as our adolescent lives move on. Always move on. And not much is learned.

Journal of the Plague Years: One

All wars are lost.
The people I face every day are not the people I face every day.
I want ecstasy but your sensible shoes lie smug at the foot of the bed.
If I could touch a face and not forget it, I could die and not regret it.
No one should have to watch their lover leave on a train.
I laugh as the shower curtain pops its hinges one by one.
The altar wavers like a mirage.
I drink the holy water and pee on the outside of the church.
I do not have one life.
He tried to salvage our relationship like it was half-burnt toast.
After Bozo retired and needles were found in Girl Scout cookies, I went into hiding.
None of this has happened.
None of this has anything to do with me.
I see your face in the moon: cheeks like windswept sand traps.
I thought we were going to have sex, but we had pork chops instead.
A day drinking: the T.V. is what I hope for most—a blur with voices somewhere near.
Always the return to you in the night like a bat to something detected in the wavy space around it.
Dreams flare like flamingos into more light.
How will I know when I arrive at the place I most desire to be?
What if you recover from your life?
What happens next is happening.
I am almost who I'm meant to be.
My head: an old house overwrought with too many dreams.
Burnt slippers on an asylum floor.
The debris is necessary.
Sometimes flotsam, sometimes something with a root.
The sun, strong old warrior, lies down in a cloudy bed of ember.
I was the river once. He was the sea.

A Month in the Country

—In this place everyone talks to their own mouth.
—Anne Sexton

I'll tell you where I am. The Dekalb Hospital Psychiatric Unit. I shook my father's hand. It doesn't make sense that we did. They locked the door after me. I don't know how I ended up here but it feels inevitable. I have a room and a roommate. His name is Tom and his mind races. He takes Stelazine for it. He is lucky, I think, to understand, unlike me, what goes on in his mind. I hold a paperback version of the New Testament. I can't recall how I got it. A dream of salvation washes over me like a wave that doesn't move me. What it means to be human: to pray when you have no other god to turn to. I dwell on when I told Susan I'd slept with a man in Carbondale. He, not Susan, stays on my mind. I have already been heavily drugged by my parents' doctor who was happy to part with handfuls of Valium. I don't know what to say so I don't speak. If it's going to be said by me, someone will have to pull it out of me somehow. Poems cry in the night. In my head a jumble of words that will one day be thrown like dice onto a page. The community room frightens me and I avoid it. The people there have nothing to do with me. They are genderless and misshapen. I cannot lift my feet enough so I shuffle in my slipper socks. We are vacuum sealed. My boat is unmoored.

Choosing Pumpkins

The colored leaves touch one another—autumn's architecture—
as we pass the many arrows pointing to roadside stands.

Midmorning we pull into Kandinsky's *Autumn in Murnau*
just off a curvy Vermont highway, the sky a smoky blue.

The requisite stuffed, starched scarecrows, witches,
and flying bats scatter among the orange pumpkins
surrounded by gnarly-shaped gourds.

The smell of the country and splashes of rustic-colored displays
make us smile as if a certain mercy had been granted to us alone.

Then there is the holding and touching, the smell of leftover dirt
on plump pumpkins and gourds oddly shaped
like creatures of myth.

We sip on steaming coffee as we paw for the perfect picks:
solid stems, flat base, bright orange hue,
the feeling it belongs in your hands.

"Every Breath You Take" plays on their speakers
and I feel suddenly sad as if smoke is filling my lungs
and I turn to you for help.

How sudden a line of poetry can take me
where I didn't know I was: "I do believe his mouth is heaven,
his kisses falling over me like stars."

Our flannel shirts touch as we pick over fall-themed items
scattered on tables—offerings to the god of orange
and rust and yellow and the smell of dying leaves,

as if all life was flotsam and driftwood washed ashore
on the hills of New England in October on the last day of our lives.

A Pound of American Flesh

—Fallujah, 2004

No women wail for the king's mercy.
No mercy.
Rotting bodies strung from telephone wire,
a ten-year-old's heel on a burned head—
the public and the profane.
At the bridge of hanging corpses
three nurses scurry at gunpoint.
In falling light, these fleeting witnesses—
bathers of babes, cocoons of hope,
the endured, the almost.

I'm Afraid by Then He Was Only Sad

There is no one left to love
Even the trees know it . . .
the dying cemetery statues
the nude descending a staircase
the hatted figure lounging in a boat
in an impressionist painting
the embalmer on his cigarette break
the least who come first
and the first who come last
or something like that
those who lie down in the wet grass for no reason
those who speak ill of the dead
the boatman
the bull's rider with his single aim
deaths that don't come in threes
the duller cardinal jealous of her red husband
those with a gauze of grief under their face
those whose ship was built to wreck
each mystery of the rosary
those in each circle of hell
me seaside, my banished sun-glassed self
awash among wasting words

If It Comes to That

—Every day you have less reason/not to give yourself away
—Wendell Berry

Each thing like something else:
the body: vessel as metaphor,
its manifest of parts.

Eyes: blue reach of water.
Your body chopping wood—a boastful ship.
Alert, you are a seagull tracking fish.

The arc of a dolphin when you stretch.
Swell of breath—what carries us through.
The pull of horizon.

Your scent: loam in a plowed field.
Sorrow heavy as the stones of cairns.
Crooked path to the old forest.

What did you mean: this shattered hope?
Do we fit in this landscape?
In the deafening dusk do I fit in *us?*

The Rite of Spring

> —*For a seed to achieve its greatest expression, it must come completely undone . . . To someone who doesn't understand growth, it would look like complete destruction.*
>
> —Cynthia Occelli

Italicized portions taken from synopses of *The Rite of Spring.*

The Adoration of the Earth

How it begins the seed stirring like a bird becoming a bird becoming more like we become more this time of year transformed by more light warmth the new alignment of the planets the equinox bending our sense of the universe around us. And in the air a new threat added to the old ones. A cold spring and damp. It's easy not to notice the daffodils, the red tulips, forsythia. *In the hills an old woman enters and begins to foretell the future.* I start out on my daily walk. The mask heats me up.

If I encounter someone without a mask on the sidewalk, I move away if they don't. Constant vigilance. It's all too much. Masks, gloves, wiping things down. It's like living in an operating room. *Young girls arrive from the river, in single file.* I nod at the postman, a weak hello. I wash my hands vigorously after taking in the mail. "Hate has no Home Here" signs stare at me from lawns, an outgrowth of the new political landscape. It's like we are living in two dystopias now, one political and one public health.

I'm continually disheartened now. Scrolling Facebook will do it. Man's inhumanity to man, that cliché literature trope. Is human nature human? I wonder sometimes. A man wiped his nose on a store employee because she asked him to wear a mask. Hundreds of stories like this. Thousands. *The People divide into two groups in opposition to each other and begin the 'Ritual of the Rival Tribes.'* Angry, armed domestic terrorists storming state capitols.

I notice two trees with tight, bright red buds that will become leaves. I want to adore the earth. *A holy procession leads to the entry of the wise elders, headed by the Sage . . . who blesses the earth.*

To gather rosebuds while I may but everything feels on hold now. These flowers, these trees frozen in their growth like my soul feels so much of the time now though I meditate twice a day searching for the way. *The people break into a passionate dance, sanctifying and becoming one with the earth.*

The Sacrifice

I want the old ways. In any form. I want to read a long, old-fashioned letter. Or write one. I cross Lombard Avenue heading toward Buzz Cafe for a to-go latte. Everything is to go now. We can't pause for long, except within the confines of our own walls that grow closer daily. At times I feel like that character in "The Tell-Tale Heart," hearing the beating, thinking I will be found out for who I am. That kind of claustrophobia. *The young girls engage in mysterious games, walking in circles.* I note the boarded-up 7-11, another economic casualty. A squirrel dashes up an old oak. I cross over the expressway and walk around Barrie Park. Yellow tape surrounds the playground. A slight mist begins. A group of soccer players kick a ball around the field. They are not supposed to be there. The parks are closed. Do I turn them in? It seems we are always monitoring others' behavior. Asking whose rights come first. *One of the girls is selected by fate . . . and is honored as the 'Chosen One' with a martial dance.* The mayor sneaked out to get a haircut without a mask. Then she threatened her citizens with arrest if they gather in large groups. So many inconsistencies, questions. I pull up my hood as the mist continues, sip my drink for warmth. Talk of snow in May. In St. Mary's we were taught to respect our elders.

So many are being rolled out on gurneys these days from nursing homes. No more than ten spaced-apart mourners can attend the service. "There will be deaths," say politicians as they panic to reopen the country. *In a brief dance, the young girls invoke the ancestors.*

In Italy they say the younger generation is now virtually without grandparents. After my three times around the park, I head back home, not just where the heart is but everything. I want that feeling of longing to be back in the warm nest of my home after a trip away instead of hunkering down in it as my place to shelter.

The Chosen One is entrusted to the care of the old wise men. What I need is someone to blame. Besides the President. In ancient Greece, human scapegoats (*pharmakos*) were used to allay a plague. We need to draw lots like in "The Lottery" and stone someone. Instead, ill winds, a frozen spring. *The Chosen One dances in the presence of the old men, in the great 'Sacrificial Dance.'*

Sent My Way

A white crow is at home in my front yard—
symbol like everything is
I know when I see a cardinal's red flit before me
It's the spirit of my mother Agnes checking in

But I didn't even know such an anomaly existed
I remember the white buffalo of Wisconsin
Many years back which drew crowds
But it died on everyone—a clear message I believe

Who likes crows to begin with
This one is loud like the rest and speaks to me
In its own inimitable bird language
A thing alone and so noticeable must be a treat

to predators—red in tooth and claw
though poets created a "murder" of crows
(scientists don't use such a term)
some primal violence is associated with them

and I wonder how many baby robins
this glorious creature by my elm has devoured
like me it must fit in with its peers where it can
It seems to feel safe and listened to with me near

When I hear a cardinal's chirp, I know God is real
When I hear this white crow, I wonder how we survive
When so much sets us apart from the flock
Our blessing, our curse

Hines VA Hospital

I didn't want to go, but father insisted.
It was Sunday and he always needed
a destination after Mass.
A man of duty—and expectation—
honor thy father and mother.

He took my brother and me—
a trip for the men in the family to visit his father
who was, once again, in the VA hospital.
I didn't know what VA stood for
and it didn't seem like a hospital.
I had only been inside once
and never wanted to return.

When we pulled in the parking lot, I begged father
to let me stay in the car.
My parents never stopped telling me
I was too sensitive but
I didn't want to see all those damaged men
in various stages of limblessness, the tubes,
puss, bags dripping medication,
to hear them moan in dark rooms, hallways.
Always have to keep an eye out for gangrene, father said.

I can't remember seeing my grandfather.
I smelled so many things I couldn't identify.
I wanted to gag, to pass out.
My brother soldiered on like he always did
knowing this had something to do with men
and duty, a chance at glory, with war
which I loved to play with my neighbor Nicky.
It was hard to believe in glory here
where no medals hung from the men's dirty robes—
my dad's Bronze Star safe in its velvet-lined box
like the coffins those who didn't survive lay in.

To Grandmothers Deceased Before My Birth

Mother's Side

Your studio portrait on my Buddhist altar:
a beautiful woman with smooth Irish skin
collar cinched high on your neck
dressed in black like a widow
as if you're prepared for your own funeral
which occurs a few days after mother's birth—
father's burial soon to follow.
Mother's memories of an orphan passed home to home,
of nothing but the damage done,
nothing to pass on to five children
but a gap in the idea of ancestry.
What she carries: a persistent without.
All I know of you, grandmother, is your absence.
How I resent your abandonment of mother
as if leaving this world was your choice.
Your lovely, framed face is all I know.

Father's Side

A workhorse is how I see you, grandmother,
scrubbing others' laundry during the Depression,
with a carpenter husband who won't take non-union jobs.
A bad heart beating, you hunch over a washtub.
It gives out when father is fighting in Europe.
Mother had good things to say about you,
having absorbed a hint of the warmth
a mother gives without thinking.
Your farm relatives in White Pigeon
stop speaking German and keep to themselves
as they did anyway, never wholly forgive
your Catholic conversion. I just know

you were a loving person who would have brought
an upholstery fabric bag full of books
to read to us, stories I will remember.

The Defiant Morning

Summer. I almost fear it.
My hand on you is confident and warm: a faint clarinet.
I'm satisfied: the marigolds on the glass stand mellow,
burnt hues like us. How bronzed our bodies are.

I fear the colors, the season of chrysanthemums even here
where marigolds, too perfect to go to seed,
bear resemblance to sunset on the sheered fields
of autumn. Dawn—silent sleuth—enters, defying us

to stay the same. What clues can you gather here?
Where everything changes. Where I am changed somehow.
You are aging, now, before my eyes, in the light of dawn,
and I think how I was never young, and here,

the morning shows: you are already old. I cannot stop this
or the morning as you throw your arm around me, as
I want to grow, but not let us go to seed.
The day expands, the old moon subjugated by something

fiercely young and hot. Daylilies, blue asters,
Queen Anne's lace turn toward it.
Each day the humidity brings the rains,
the rumbling of an advancing enemy.

Each afternoon I ready a bucket for the trailer roof's leak.
I will spend much of my life in poorly constructed tenements,
lowering windows, sopping up water,
making love on a damp mattress. Amid the flashes, thunder,

the driving rains, we touch. Afterward, the calm,
the cooler breeze, the quiet—time stopped to get its bearings—
and I mine. I must leave here soon.
A new sun rises upon our flesh,

as you lie here unwrapped, naked to the onset of cooler mornings.
How can it be, how can it be
there are other men outside this door,
other summers we will travel apart?

Waiting to Grow up

—includes answers to some most asked questions on Google

We had tuna casserole almost every Friday. That or scrambled eggs. Or fish sticks which made me gag. Sunday evenings my parents would unveil a half gallon of Neapolitan ice cream and slice it in pieces to put between fresh, hot-off-the-griddle waffles. This was the kindest thing they ever did. It's not like we dined on beef stroganoff or even knew what it was. Although a relative once brought rabbit for us to cook for Sunday dinner. I had mixed feelings about that even then. Mother could turn anything—a wrinkle in time—into a casserole. And we'd eat it. She never stopped moving. It's not like someone would be waiting at the door at day's end carrying a dozen roses for all her efforts. And she never stopped warning us of things. If we laid out in the sun too long, she said get inside you'll get sunstroke. She believed this. Our grandfather's brother spent his life in an asylum and they'd diagnosed him with sunstroke, so she imagined us babbling in some dark ward somewhere from too much sun. Every Sunday at mass I stared at the statue of the Virgin Mary and thought of sky. I saw blue everywhere for a while. Let silence take you to the core of life. Rumi said this but I sensed the truth of it after Communion. Still, I resented being so small and unheard I could never plan what to do next. I went with the flow.

What to Do with Entirely?

—with fragments from Sylvia Plath's "The Colossus"

No sense looking for an oracle here

A voice says look at the other:
the hydrangea, blue-blush like a new color
inside me born through my O-shaped mouth

Disaster blooms everywhere and I'm no wiser

My soul bruised: the little children of Syria gassed
takes away your heart that sings with the daily joys
I hoard when I should be mourning

Kissing your worried brow
hoping it will all clear if we learn
a new way to see with our eyes
You lost in yourself, your own Roman Forum
We search for one another in a forest of cypress

What to do with entirely?
A world of woe littered around us
to the horizon-line: the dead Crimeans
terrorized Parisians
the runners the Russians the ruin

But here before me an azalea plum-colored,
freshly ground Lavazza, sun through my east windows
taste of honey-dipped brioche on my tongue

The world as it is only a shadow
my body an invisible keel
taking me to yet another landing

It is not right when a random bomb is
waiting to go off, singing.

Miss Willoughby

—portrait of a young girl by George Romney, 18th Century,
in the National Gallery, Washington

Posed before a British landscape
pink cherub face smooth
hat large as sky tilts her head
as she fusses with its pink ribbons
full fingers on one so young
a matching sash around her waist
herself, sky, trees, earth splash on canvas
with a simple palette: red, yellow, and blue
a pale picture, a child, an ivory dress
the natural world behind flows like time
she will not be able to arrest

The artist hesitant to paint one
so petulant and young, Juliana forced
to stand at her mother's command told
to be still repeatedly
thinking only of Sasha
her pony waiting in the stalls
as she waits for this to end
her one victory the lack of a smile
to please her mother who frets
among the heavy velvet drapes
where Mr. Romney's eyes appeal to her

I remember the studio portraits we sat for
in the fifties and sixties our parents proud
of their carefully posed children
in church clothes and freshly polished shoes
my beefy brother, the oldest, anchors one end
our baby sister the other: a lopsided see-saw
I squirm in the middle of five

unnerved by the lights
caught in time we are developed
as black and white photos
to be smudged by our relatives' hands

Little Nude by Table

—painting by Henry Strater, 1925

Wild hair—roughly cut, bob worn.
Weak lips, brow surprised,
arms as if bound behind.
One hand grips a robe
landing at the floor in waves—
pink-orange breasts,
belly button's shadow,
"v" balancing the body,
feet—solid anchors for hips.
She waits for him to trap her,
finally,
to let her grow.

Fugue State

I remember climbing the ladder to the top bunk, my older brother beneath. Not rough like him, I was much finer sandpaper. He terrified me by saying the Klan hated Catholics and they might come after us. I remember trying to hear him breathe, wanting to lie beside him. How he flexed his biceps and strutted around in his underwear. How he taught me to do a paper route, let me play H-O-R-S-E though I almost never made a basket. We shared the same bed. I remember the danger of his side by mine. The waking up. The forgetting. I remember when I completely stopped speaking to him, the darkness which frightened me before I fell asleep. His solid presence a weight I would always carry. I remember when he went off to war, when he read Mao's little red book, brought a college art textbook home and I was aroused by Picasso's angular naked women. His weaving in and out on the expressway taking me to therapy. I remember my brother as a landscape I almost escaped.

Design

—after *The Women He's Undressed,* documentary about Orry-Kelly, three-time Oscar winning costume designer

How to solve a problem like Bette's breasts
Hanging like fruit almost to the waist?
(She thought wire support caused cancer.)
Or how to make the ball gown in Jezebel
Appear to be red using black and white?
You did the impossible with layers,
Types and sheerness of fabric, ingenuity.
The cheek of making Marilyn appear nude,
Breasts overflowing, resting on air,
Censors shocked into submission.
Toning down Ros Russell's outfits
For the serious scenes while running amok
With wacky designs for her dynamo ones,
Her Mame a force blasting the Hollywood screen.

Behind the scene you worked your sleight of hand
brought the real and the illusory to a waiting audience,
But refused the ruse that you preferred women.
Archie Leach/Cary Grant never rose to the occasion
As your friend, so enamored with fame and posterity
Hiding like so many did then.
Three times you took Oscar home like a trick,
A queer conquering fear in a dangerous time.
You show them it can be done like
the magic you perform with tulle, linen, and silk
to wrap your leading ladies. A design for living—

Weekly Ritual

I had three sisters and a mother and none of them went to beauty parlors. I felt cheated by not being able to vicariously experience their visits. I'd have liked to have seen what could have been done to their hair for I had my own ideas. So many possibilities swirling like a beehive do in my head. When my mother was ancient, she took a friend religiously to her hair appointment. The woman had god-awful, dyed black hair and looked the same after she came out. Mother never did something because others did. In this case I wish she had. I lost out on all that gossip women bathed each other in that I witnessed in movies and on TV. I figured these parlors were the newsiest places on earth. Perhaps if I'd known a grandmother, she would have run a beauty salon and I could have hung out there with all the heavily scented women who wandered out with immovable hair.

Let Your Hair Down

. . . and only as she dreamt of the yellow hair
did moonlight sift into her mouth
—"Rapunzel" from *Transformations* by Anne Sexton

yellow hair
straw into gold
words into art

suffering—always that—
other stories too:

the long tail of myth
each archetype
a nugget:

the young breast—
the old—
the witch's garden

Rapunzel—beautiful
girl in a locked tower
the prince

(Rapunzel, Rapunzel)
his dancing stick (ha!)
finally

her tears
on his blind eyes
the happily living
after

the old woman
her dreams of gold

Family Tree

—That's what it means to be crazy.
Those I loved best died of it—the fool's disease.
—Anne Sexton

Why did she have to surrender both brother and son? Who took them to the state asylum? What was the weather like those days? Did they think they would see home again? Did anyone speak?

Did anyone ask them how they felt? What did they wear? Did they imagine what tomorrow would be like? The day after? The day after that?

Why did father lie in bed for weeks when he should have been in school? What kind of sick was he? What made someone like this? What did the term "scrupulosity" mean? Did it have something to do with his worrying about whether he had committed a sin? What kind of doctor could cure this?

Why did mother tell us to come in out of the sun when we sunbathed for too long? *You'll get sunstroke like those crazy relatives of your father in the asylum?* Was sunstroke even a thing? Was it code for madness? Was she really afraid of a return trip to Mercy Psychiatric Center where she went after threatening to kill me as an infant? How did shock therapy feel? Being jolted by insulin injections, cold water sprayed on her . . . how much did she forget after her treatments? For how long?

Did she picture me in Aunt Esther's protective arms? Why did she attack Esther after being released, screaming, *You're trying to steal my baby!* when she'd wanted to throw me away? Who saved me? My father? Esther? Have I been saved?

Why did I shake my father's hand like a businessman when he gave me to the psych ward? What lay behind that locked door? Why did the sound of cicadas in late summer make me so depressed? Where did I get the modern translation of the New Testament I had on me? Why could no one here help me? How did I get so deep inside myself? Who could bring me out?

How do I unravel the threads of insanity, the roots of our family tree binding me to earth? Is that why I dreamed so much of flying as a child? To escape those roots? Did I know then how harm stays, how long the reach of the past is?

Slouching Toward Spring: A Pantoum

The cat lies belly up in the sun's warmth.
The amaryllis has given up the ghost.
Somewhere the sounds of childhood echo.
I have come too far to falter now.

The amaryllis has given up the ghost.
I am a traveler without a Baedeker.
I have come too far to doubt now.
Winter spreads its fingers into the end of March.

We are travelers who think we have agendas.
Crocuses feel crushed below.
We still put our fingers resentfully into gloves.
Seasons should soothe our needs.

Crocuses feel crushed below.
Older now, I attune myself to hear kind words.
Seasons are primal and indifferent.
My legs are a fortress for my cat to rub against.

Many are kinder now to an older gentleman.
The challenge is to live with so many gone.
I am a seaport for my cat's electric fur.
Warmth is what I most desire.

With so many gone I mourn daily.
Nothing mitigates.
Warmth is what we most desire.
I am grateful for the light on water.

Nothing mitigates.
Sometime I feel I chose this life.
I am grateful for the quiet evening.
If winter comes . . .

Sometimes I feel I had no say in this life.
My great aunt Bertha smelled like dough.
If winter comes . . .
My people taught me to prevail.

My great aunt Bertha put a penny in my palm as goodbye.
At least some birds are singing now.
My people taught me to prevail.
The ocean I love is so far away.

At least some birds are singing now.
I hope my parents got new, separate lives.
The ocean I love is within me.
The cat lies belly up in the sun's warmth.

P is for Picasso

P is for police—an explosive word now—a bomb.
P is for primrose which sounds very English though I don't know if it is.
P is for Provincetown which has sand and vivid wildflowers, water, horizon, and lots of gay sex and drugs.
P is for prominent like Churchill's nose.
P is for permanent, the smell scorching my nostrils when my mother or sister took over the kitchen sink.
P is for permanent—how my mistakes feel.
P is for poodle, the silliest quadruped.
P is for pomegranate—an object you should always put in a poem.
P is for Percival which also sounds English and I'm pretty sure it is.
P is for Picasso who answered when someone said, "There are more important things in life than art," "No, not to me."
P is for plantain which a white boy knew nothing about.
P is for pending, another word for life.
P is for post-partum depression, the hole into which my mother fell after my birth.
P is for popular, something I never was or will be.
P is for the portraits of Gertrude Stein and the Mona Lisa, two women who made an impression.

P is for private dancer, one of the saddest songs ever.

P is for Portuguese. The fisherman I almost loved in Provincetown.

P is for priest but not for purity.

P is for penultimate which this line is.

P is for posthumous. I have nothing to say about that.

Summer Children of New England

Perfect shells
polished.

Sun-warmed,
lightly starched.

Freed from insignias,
caps turned back,

boys wild for crab flats,
cold, cocky surf.

Teenage girls, scented like honeysuckle,
shop for shiny things,

amphibious both on the streets
and in locked bedrooms.

Morning sand for hair,
ocean eyes, skin of white violets.

What Does It Take to Be Happy?

I imagine you and me rowing a boat. Then would you talk to me as we face one another directly? Will the water rippling off the hull please you? The blue sky and the sight of green forest on the shores? You don't have to believe in God to see something more than what is there. As a child I saw a hummingbird and couldn't breathe in astonishment. I couldn't move that fast and wondered why. I rushed to my mother excited. Has anything like this happened to you? You're actually putting some effort now in rowing our boat and we actually have a sort of rhythm. You almost look content. Are we now bonding in a way similar to trust exercises at a retreat? (Was it something I said? The way I dressed? Was I politically incorrect? I have my bad days too. Weren't you taught to give everyone the benefit of the doubt like I was, though I could never really do it.) *The weather is perfect,* I say hoping to crack open silence, knowing you'll find this remark completely banal. *You make a great Canadian latte, I add.* I can barely tell, but I think I see a tiny smile leak like intimacy through a small crack in our boat.

Recipe for an Execution

—Utah, 2010

5 rifles, 4 with live ammo,
1 with a blank.
Each of us takes one and assumes positions.

In the desert blood smelled like rust,
in the city its smell mingled with that of
hanging meat, cumin, baharat, teens' lust

The condemned man strapped to the chair, faceless.
I know his story, his media face.

Someone has to play God

We stand 20 feet back with our 30 caliber
rifles aimed at the target drawn over his 1 heart.

Danny down in the backstreet arm dangling
bleeding out

Signal given, we do our duty,
not knowing if our shot was a killing shot.

I hope mine was.

I don't need a blank for my conscience.

There's a right way to live.
A right way to die.
And plenty of ammunition.

The Lover of Horses . . .

waits for them to be let into the field,
crests flashing light in the still, autumn dawn

sits in her poster-filled bedroom sketching the creature she rides
Tuesday and Thursday, in love with its gentle power its brown eyes

picks the hooves, uses a curry comb to remove loose hair,
brushes the mane and tail, smoothes warmth into its flanks

is the convict learning to tame a wild mustang
speaking a language that soothes them both

includes a sensitive boy hesitantly offering sugar cubes to
the mare hesitantly approaching his outstretched hand

finds Degas at the racecourse sketching
the movement and grace of each brown beauty

is the crooked man who helps rebuild stalls at Maywood Track
after the fire in which he helped them escape into air

gets a glimpse of the wild ones galloping
through a Nevada morning like a late-for-work dream

Nocturne on the North Shore

We sense Lake Michigan breathing behind mansions, joke every time about the line from *Doctor Zhivago* where the official says fourteen families could live in such a large house. We want to share more as we walk the streets of Evanston barely lit by the muted historic streetlamps. I didn't know then how much you meant. I wanted as a child still—any shiny, moving thing. But you are becoming a poem I can't memorize twirling in my head, throbbing. Being so young, you open yourself more easily—a shaft of light I barely see in the limelight of my wanting to glow myself. When I say I have to go home, your face falls. I never pass up an opportunity to distance myself, to hide in the darkness swallowing Sheridan Road as you hang your head and I try to fathom, but don't, the depth of your disappointment. I can't imagine anyone feeling they want to be with me that badly. We imagine the waves here on the perfect, lonely sidewalk. When we part, the night paws at my leg like a needy dog. I picture you hugging the pillow you want to belong to me.

Journal of the Plague Years: Two

I pick words like fruit, feeling for those most pregnant with
meaning but not already having meant.
A man is an island. How to guard on so many fronts?
What mad king has torn out his eyes this time?
Will we love one another again?
The sudden dip of gulls along the rocky shore.
Boats with names dock in Halifax Harbor.
The Bay of Fundy's lonely sweep.
The whole story is not whole.
Antidepressants ruined art—what greatness is culled by the easy
pill?
Adele Hugo collapses on the sands of Barbados—when love
becomes madness: as unclear as sky versus water on the
horizon.
The more sex I have, the more I get even.
Perhaps the gulls will refuse to be painted.
Perhaps they already have.
You may be all I know of God.
I feel stuck in that time in which most accidents occur.
Put me to bed like a child who's been disappointed.
They've linked hair chemistry to violence but have no idea, yet,
how two people love, or fail to.
This is what we can give one another: the silent pain
of ancient sculptures without hands.
Right now, make small talk. Please.

White Rooms

The playthings on the beach looked cold.
A boat was upside down.
She said they saved people in summer.
I bought a radio with my own money.
I thought I would swim there.
She only let me play it sometimes.
Some kids tried to steal it I ran and made it home.
It was raining and I wish it was summer.

I'm afraid of the house behind the tavern.
The walls are white and rough.
There is nothing in the rooms.
Some men did bad things to me.

She bought me a swimming suit.
I tried it on.
After dinner she cut it up with big blue scissors.
Then she cut off her hair and burned it in a dish.

She sat and made clothes with needles.
I had a nice new sweater.
She prayed a lot and read to me from a big book.
She wore a rug and said sin was bad like men in white rooms.

It was hot.
She dressed me for swimming.
She still wore heavy things.
She sat with me outside the fence.
I watched everyone swimming.
They threw water at each other.

I have never been swimming.
She caught me trying to sneak in.
She burned my hand.
When it was all better she gave me back.
I don’t live in a house by the lake.
I play my radio sometimes.

Shifting

—after *The Sheltering Sky:*
book by Paul Bowles and film by Bernardo Bertolucci

There are many ways to abandon oneself.
How did Kit come to be here in the desert
content to leave behind her American self.
She bounces on a camel's back,
existential blankness on her browning face.
A bright hijab wraps her head and neck,
desert winds to no effect as she is full with heat.

Her husband, Port, deserts her by dying
at a Foreign Legion post in the North African desert,
sands shifting as she stares out the one window.
He insisted they were travelers, not tourists.
Fine distinctions worthless to her now
having deserted her old culture, her old self.
Is she becoming someone else or no one?

Soon her Bedouin lifestyle, her young,
new lover take her to a world of forgetting, her grief
expressed in one breath, sensual delight in another,
unsure if she's being held captive as they fuck—
identity a fluid thing.

Her old elite crowd talked and talked.
How little language matters,
though she and her brown lover share the names
of body parts in their languages.
She can't stop moving.

By chance, arriving back to where she and Port started,
tattooed, nearly catatonic—a mud pot—all form,

an American former friend (for she is friendless)
finds her and arranges a journey back to the states
but she refuses, also countryless now
she moves back into sand settling behind her,
pathless, a traveler under the sheltering sky.

The Scent of the Sea

Imagine a begonia, an artichoke, the breath of an iron lung,
the moment you believe in solace to smooth yourself.
Today you walk the steep cliffs where hikers
trod the paths of slow generations; memory is want.
Even a step is risky: a riptide in the wrinkle of time.
A forgotten insult, an amulet, a scattering of crows.
Because a melody I hum this morning has cinders and sparks,
a blue flame of inspiration to echo, an element undiscovered.
But I discover nonetheless, a gem polished
between the unfinished prelude for cellos
and the hope that in heaven, for instance,
a boulevard welcomes heretics like desert its just-in-time shower.

It Has Come to That

It has been a year. I vent on Facebook. I got punished for one of my posts, banned by the Facebook censors for twenty-four hours. Feelings are running high. I felt like I'd been sent to my room at the age of sixty-something. I've had groceries delivered for months now. These are my memories of shopping at the start of the pandemic: In and out is the goal. I tighten my mask over my nose. No pausing over whether to buy generic or the real brand. Grab at what strikes me first. No pausing in the pet supplies aisle where I want to linger because I've had my cat put down after eighteen years. I must focus. I'm on a mission even as I tear up at the thought of the needle in her leg's vein that ended it all. My petting her with gloves on, how I wanted to really feel her soft, furry head as I said, "It's okay, Maggie." If only I could see someone smile at some small kindness. I would feel buoyed. Do I need mouthwash? Who would notice if I have bad breath? I want my life back. I drive through Dunkin Donuts and get an oat milk iced latte before I cruise around town in my new red Volvo with the moon roof open, the radio loud. A new pandemic ritual. I'm a teenager again with no particular place to go.

A Painted Lady Can Be a House or a Butterfly

Paired samaras of the Boxelder   float to ground.
The concept of samsara taught by Buddha   includes our sufferings.
What everybody asks   is where did it all start.
If life never ends   it continues not begins.
Must there be an original   prime motion.
Where did it gain velocity and thrust   become us?
Perhaps it started   with a black box of code,
A spark, a bang   a membrane breeched.
Perhaps the milking room   is where it all began,
The smell of udders freshly   squeezed.
Or with the scent of   the sea moving westward
Creatures evolved to explore land. A divination in the desert,
In the contents of a seedpod   a bulb in the earth full of lust.

Unbelievers use ellipses more than believers Altruists forego controversy for haloed vowels (stamen, pistil, heresy, Puritan) Drone strikes and kestrels rule the sky What we believe starts every war (an autobahn of trochees) Manure reanimates The half-moon leaflets of moonwort green with chlorophyll: a veneration *Face facts* someone was always saying (no need to say someone is always left out) Especially the praying mantis The names of the full moons will replace poetry Skin cells have better memory than I (shale, catastrophe, shagbark) Conjure an ending here or go on

Mother of IRA Leader Tries to Bury Her Son

My feet don't fail me.

Morning, we start again, casket raised above the crowd.

We push forward, troops drive us back.

I want a place for him to finally die.

Each evening my hands pray, *tomorrow.*

They shout hero's chants—I reach for the hard shell that holds him.

I want to kneel at his grave and forgive no one.

They claim him for themselves, but I loved him before reason.

Realms: Demeter and Persephone

1.

how fast we can
be borne below,
sunlight a memory,
a flutter of blue,
home divisible by two,
catastrophe? abyss?
a husk Persephone
must inhabit? a lesser myth
would end here:
instead a queen
of impermanence;
far from home,
there is no choice,
even Zeus can't
withstand a mother's
thirst for daughter/
            a new covenant
            warms the fallow land,
            the deaf
            dusk of April
            stirs the noteless songbird

2.

a god in a sudden chariot
takes her to a sunless space—
death and the maiden—
beside him she smiles
at the victory of separating

from her mother/not knowing
six pomegranate seeds in her palm
will divide her in two/
he keeps her for all futures
for half a year but
never wholly conquers/
not on Olympus
his only power is to keep souls
below/his love
of suffering is a container
holding water, futility,
thirst; another force
works through earth
to air above; that
which can't be stilled.

3.

a mother grieves,
herself a goddess,
knows a lonely Hades was dangerous,
for a man takes what he wants
always/a barren earth
within her power, no violets fall
from her daughter's apron/a new deal
when day's light grows longer:
lavender-blue
jacaranda, fingertips
soft against bark,
scent of loam,
all that holds us
here to the swelling
hill.

One Life

—You're always one decision away from a totally different life.
—Anonymous

Covered with ice packs, she sprawls on a white sheet.
Skin blisters. A fan whispers her boyfriend's name,

tells her how skin will shed—delicate membranes—layer by layer.
She waits, pictures herself a bride.

Yes, she said *I do* but blood drained from her face
and abdication churned in her. No day had been holy since then.

Who was she after the diaper changes, the plates stacked
on granite counters? What she longs for most is herself

as she leaves everything: husband, four children.
She cries into a bucket of golf balls; with growing force

she hits each one, hears the solid slap of steel, rushed parting of air.
She cooks for an ever-changing family of artists and writers.

Food is her medium. She blends flavors as pigments,
dyes, creates with asparagus tips, artichoke hearts, warm bread,

and aspic, listens to lofty discussions on books, art,
the creative process, placates everyone's quirks, demands, egos.

She smiles—a perfect hostess is what they want,
no different from her family. Always the giving,

the smoothing over: *it will be alright.*
Now she lives in a high rise by the Atlantic, lounges at a Tiki bar,

drives her convertible up and down A1A,
swims laps in a thunderstorm because she can.

On Any Given Day You Are

An upside-down baseball cap—a turtle on its back
Blue cloth napkins folded sails on plates in a Greek restaurant
White hydrangeas craving water
Heartbreak in a child over the canceled birthday party
A pot-bound peace plant reaching for more room
As trendy as torn-up jeans with ripped pockets
Picasso in his striped shirt with palms on the window glass
A curio cabinet added to after each new death
A tiny silver pitcher of cream on a silver tray a la Vienna
Quebec's motto: *je me souviens*
Watercolor paintings on red and yellow walls
The rowboat that flows through toddlers' stories
The hard-to-get-at sweetness of sugarcane
Yellow lilies and blue iris exciting suburban yards
Heat from a tinfoil tan reflector held under the chin
My confidence in someone else's flight plan

Indochine

—after French film starring Catherine Deneuve

I should have fled but nothing existed but him, Eliane thinks.
They make love in the back of a chauffeured car,
in her childhood home in Saigon.
Jean-Baptiste stifled by this small arrangement, his posting:
I want to discover the world.

As funeral boats bob in thick mist and fog, Eliane holds Camille's
hand, the Asian girl she will raise on her rubber plantation.
Though French, Eliane says, *I am Asian,*
calls her Indochine workers "coolies."

Camille, sheltered by Eliane from native unrest,
from larger ideas, from love,
is rescued by Jean-Baptiste from a shooting on the street
and sees him as her handsome knight in naval uniform.
If I don't marry him I'll die.
She takes off alone to Dragon Island where he's been banished,

walks for weeks to the sea, to where coolies are traded
as slaves for the empire. Eliane thinks:
Now she has Indochine inside her.
Camille shoots a French officer and she and Jean-Baptiste flee.
He hears Eliane's voice: *You won't be able to resist her.*
She's irresistible.
Their infant son in tow, they escape authorities for a time.

Eliane, a part of herself now, lies on flat beds in opium dens
like a commoner. Camille's matchmaker is devout and practical:
I'll never understand French peoples' love stories . . .
Just like our war stories.

Camille, sent to prison, becomes a communist
destined to help form a free Vietnam.
Eliane gets custody of their son, holds him tight.
Jean-Baptiste visits Eliane before his court martial,
spends the night in her family's old home, tiny Etienne beside him.

The Popular Front frees all political prisoners.
Eliane is there among the horde, but the reunion
with her daughter is not as she expected.
Camille asks about the child but her own pain is too great.
It's too late, Maman. I have no past. I've forgotten everything.
Your Indochine is no more. It's dead.

Women in Movies

Don't know themselves. The man making the movie has seen too many movies with such women: the femme fatale, the whore, the prostitute, the loud-mouth, bossy shrew (*Who's Afraid of Virginia Woolf?*), the woman's libber, the artist going her own way, the users of men who sleep with their professors, their casting director, their Olympic trainer, anyone in authority. And there's always the part in the plot where the woman we've been trusting turns on someone, usually a man who's in love with her. You can count on her having her own secret agenda. In French films women are more unique and unpredictable. They sometimes completely lose their sense of self over a passionate obsession which isn't really love but they are past the point of recognizing this. They surprise with irrational sometimes violent actions and reactions saying words that don't match how their lips move. This is why they get so many close-ups like Jean Seberg in her new-wave self. Why Huppert initiates rough sex in a bathroom, and Deneuve stands stately on a funeral boat in Indochina. Here in America, Lana Turner's confident hand signs her confession with a bold X and Blanchett purrs like a feline under her red wool coat ready to pounce.

Silent Movie

In a previous life I could not hear
Not even a breathy hint of sound
Not even

I imagined the roar of a waterfall
You calling me through spray
Me a car on a foggy mountain road

Now the confused ash tree sways two directions
Now a song sings somewhere
As your body echoes next to mine
A cacophony of consonants stilled
Your drowsy penis a star in a constellation
Cocooned in silk sheets the color of butter

The moon a piano played by a river of clouds
We make love again and it's new
You hold me like you're saving me from drowning
Swim knowingly toward shore

What my body holds back is not betrayal
A fear of floating on my back without your supporting arms

You make me want to hold every word in
You make me want to tell it all

Knowledge

What is your poetry about?
I don't know.
The sound of a loon soaring over the bay?

The Pablum on my baby spoon?
I don't know how the universe propels itself
or how it touches what I do, what I write.

I want to be an expert botanist who understands
the signature of all things in the natural world.
I want to read the environment, transcribe it into words.

I don't know how Mary Oliver did it but I'm her disciple looking
for clues in her work, in her beloved Provincetown.
I don't know how much we need to *understand,*

or what kind of understanding, or if we just examine ourselves
in search of small truths not the eternal ones:
Beauty is truth, Truth Beauty.

It is in the striving to mimic genius that I am caught though:
this battered soul, this dissolving body. I don't know
why autumn is so beautiful or why I want each season inside me.

The leaves are falling like snow over Ireland.
I know that now never seems to be enough.
I know that now is enough.

Disciple

—after Mary Oliver

Pencils hidden in trees in case something speaks to her,
in case she is urged to respond as she wanders forest, seashore—
this patch of Province Lands packed with emblems.

'Listen, are you breathing just a little, and calling it a life?'

A disciple of Thoreau—world as cipher, subtext:
the disquieted deer, seven white butterflies,
watchful owl, battered whelk,
the world's roots, what lies under?

'Graced as it is with the ordinary.'

It is sweet to wake each day, to taste sea spray,
smell the fecund earth, feel birch bark,

'You are the heart of the cedars of Lebanon and the fir
called Douglas, the bristlecone, the willow.'

fit onto a meditation seat of moss,
hear the cacophony of birdsong, ocean splash.

'I dream at night of the birds, of the beautiful dark seas
they push through.'

It is not a wide range of space that matters,
but what each part means to the whole, to the human soul.
Blackwater Pond is life—dross, infinite, random.

'Tell me what is it you plan to do with your one wild and
precious life?'

Stilled in each moment noting connections in this palette of the varied.

'Luminous as it is with mystery and pain.'

Not human society but permutations of God:
marsh lily, gull, the Truro bear.

'There is only one question: how to love this world?'

Moments one knows what it is to be alive
fully and willing to live fully in the moment.

'Morning by singular morning and shell by broken shell.'

Lauderdale

Shirtless, young volleyball players eager to be seen stretch every muscle to the sound of construction rigs in wind. I thought I'd be sure of so much by the time I was this old. Hypnotized by the palms' sway, that blue sky and white building haze, is there still time for my words to matter? The older men cavort like teenagers on the gay beach off Sebastian Boulevard. I think of *Death in Venice* when I see a stunning, blonde youth saunter by. There is always time I think. We all matter. Don't we? I turn onto Birch Road where I know the names of resorts lined up sharing walls. I buzz myself in, jealous of the hushed voices of a couple in Speedos. Will I ever be happy for others? Will I ever join in? A gecko scurries into brush. The pride flag waves high above the pool. In my perfect room the A/C drones like contentment. Anonymous tourists slather on sunscreen as the scents of the tropics reach me here. The smell of chlorine lingers as I doze over my journal poolside. Listening to others laugh during happy hour, I keep myself to myself. The stray calico cries into dusk. Luxury cars cruise oceanfront along A1A. Turtles nest in sand. Orchids cling. Surfboards and beach chairs are stacked. Beachwear peels from bodies as skin stings with heat all over Florida. I've not been mistaken all this time.

The Reward

Boston bomber Tsarnaev's statement scribbled inside boat riddled with bullet holes and streaks of his blood

I'm jealous of my brother
(inshallah) before me. do not mourn his
soul God has a plan for each person. Mine was
to hide in his boat I ask Allah
to allow me to return to him
in the high levels of heaven.

Allah guides

no God but Allah

The U.S.
Government is killing innocent
civilians you
know that.
such evil
Muslims are one body
you hurt us all

the ummah is beginning
the mujahideen are
fighting men who look into the barrel of your
gun and see heaven, now how can you compete
with that.

Illinois: The Prairie State: The Wildflowers

—Wildflowers, as well as their habitats, tend to be fragile. In general, such flowers are seldom suited for bouquets. They are better left growing as nature intended and preserved by memory or photograph.
—Wildflowers of Illinois Woodlands by Runkel and Bull

Heart-of-the-
earth, Birth-
root.
Lillium, Lonicera, French willow
herb.
Orange root, Oxalis,
Oswego tea.
Bittersweet, Boneset, Celadine.
Poison ash, Hepatica.
Prairie fire, Puffball, Queen-
of-the-meadow.
Rock lily, Rosa, Rue
anemone.
Milkmaids, Moonseed, Shooting star.
Sweet slumber, Sea
sedge, Sweet
anise. Spring orchis, Trillium, Trumpet
ash. Wakerobin, Wapatoo,
Whippoor-
will shoe. Wickawee, Bloodroot,
Indian apple. Cloistered heart,
Touch-me-
not. Shame face,
Yarrow, Widow's frill. Venus cup.
Love knot, Angelica, Bleeding
heart.

The Blind Leading the Blind

Sometimes I didn't understand where my father wanted me to shine it. He swore. I didn't know the names of engine parts or tools. What kind of son was I anyway? I had no idea what was wrong with the car now. He was always swearing. It was clear life was a battle. Holding the flashlight for him was an honor as he didn't think I was much good at anything—being given to flights of fancy and nose always in a book. But it also proved his point because I wasn't much good at holding the light either. I got so bored I let it stray. This task was a microcosm of our relationship. I must have wanted to please him at some point. I can't remember that far back to a time before he doused my spark of love for him. I got it back later in life when he needed me in a much larger way. I also finally realized that he wasn't much good as a mechanic either, that I'd assumed he knew what he was doing. That was a long time ago when we were a young family in the house at the top of a hill on Home Street. Where the heart is. Or where it is, in theory.

The Centre Cannot Hold

—*Diary of Anne Frank*, April 14, 1944

I wish for so much, she wrote
when there was not much left but wishes.

She knows one who complained about
measuring out his life with coffee spoons,

but she can remember her panoramic life.
Nothing's connected anymore.

What does a century mean after all?
We tell ourselves the same things no matter when.

She wrote that her diary wouldn't matter much.
Yet how she must have surprised herself on the page,

something every writer aims for:
anger at her mother, feelings for Peter.

During this shelter in place I think of her
as many ignore restrictions.

How dangerous does the world have to be before
some realize all of us matter—Jews, the disabled?

If only it was all over, she wrote. If only.
This is a dark world with a rare flash of sun on water

where we must, at all times, keep our distance from one another.
Like her father said: *This is how we must live, until it's over.*

Sometime a Bunny Is Only . . .

—The writer Sabra Embury has spent a decade collecting 10-second drawings of rabbits from some of the most esteemed names in literature
—from an article in *The New York Times*

It begins as a parlor game: asking writers to draw bunnies,
pass them around to see if guests can guess who drew which one

like hiring a psychic or palm reader only letting
those present think they have psychological insight to the writers/

Later she asks writers at book signings to take ten seconds
to draw a bunny alongside their autograph

Of course, Atwood takes the prize with her
female rabbit holding up a carrot like a feminist torch/

But there are other runners-up like Joy Williams's dog
chasing a barely perceptible creature (the work of art?)/

perhaps the amount of time a writer has to capture *le bon mot*?
How psychoanalytical should we get with something so silly?

If anything is really silly (ask the psychotherapist)/
Note Shteyngart's hare with ears like Einstein's hair on

a man's body electrified after a psychotic break (has he seen
a rabbit?)/Inside *House of Leaves* nearly a full page of ears

the rest scribbles of swirls: a body, a tail, a totally separate nose/
Lethem's chubby bunny balanced, pleased and sated

(like the reader after experiencing *Motherless Brooklyn*?)/
David Lynch at first plays it safe: tall, thin ears, but then

some other creature's long nose, a thick un-rabbit like tail,
the whole thing standing at attention: (alert as his imagination?)

Elements

—cento from my poetry collection *The Way Here* by Aldrich Press

/Land/
Warm bricks wrapped against the frozen light
In the wings of my hands/heavy grapes
        Tourists look up/goldfish ready for feeding
The embrace of earth/dirt cool on a bulb's skin/on mine
Anonymous face of an Amish doll/in this country
        now and then/the same

Sough of wildflowers in wind/the fecund tomb of night
Geese fly into formation/wild grasses fade
        nothing I say matters
How alone the moon looks
What happens next is happening
        Have I prayed to the wrong god?

/Water/
        Anything/begins with water: cell, tributary, heart
In the rushes gently rocking/the insects' hum/a lullaby
I pulled him out of the water
        I am not who you think I am/not who I thought I was/
not who I was meant to be
Currents free seaweed/my palms feel hollow/I send you away

        Sea like the frameless landscape of Illinois
It is I who separates this world from the next
Lanterns, fires dot shoreline/I did not want to let you go
        I leave behind even less than I think
The stars/strung on boats in the canals
A palette of fish filled with light

        There is no one left to love

I hear orchids grow in wet seclusion
Life, like anything, is a habit
        can be found almost anywhere, can happen to anyone
Take me as I am
We will leave no trace upon the battered shore

Three Fridas

—a photograph by Nickolas Muray of Frida Kahlo
as she paints *Las Dos Fridas*

Frida, bright red flowers in her hair,
head tilted, off-white earrings dangling
pauses to look at Nickolas/

brush and paint-blotched palette
in her left hand, she is two places at once:
caught on film in this snapshot moment

and the next stroke of her brush moving in her mind,
the large canvas of *Las Dos Fridas*
behind her, two stately-postured versions of herself

holding hands, clouds in a dark blue sky behind/
Nickolas wonders at the three Fridas before him
at the striking woman paused on her stool

the other two of her sitting in front of sky/
it is too much!
these many versions of one/

does holding hands prevent disappearing into clouds?
her painted selves live in her mind freely
till anchored in paint and canvas

Nickolas is confused for a moment
Which Frida is real?

Lineage

—after Marjorie Stelmach's "Canticle of Want"

Lord of souvenir shops in old Western towns; of fake leather
holsters, feathered Apache headbands; Lord of flesh and bone, of

pulsing arteries, of the anatomy of grief; of fumaroles and solar
flares;
    Lord of the poppy field, of opium dens, of the impregnating
    seed;

of crows' curses and the evil eye; of the forged identity card,
of the anonymous refugee, of the warfare trenches
    redolent with earthsmell;

Lord of Lisbon's beauty, embroidery's accretion of detail; of
cornsilk and unhealed
    wounds; of the owl forced to fly from loggers; of the
lightless canyon and underwater caves, the graceful eel;

Lord of rosemary and healing linden leaves; the canticle of the
Magnificat, her blue wings, the cherubim.

At times peril sustains us: an irony not lost on the saved.
    Bells rung as a call to prayer ignored by the unbeliever as

he curses the broken vows common as rotting apples.
    A tulip bulb is placed gently in a hole, for what beauty
    comes to us

    comes later. Furrows of dug-up earth take what seeds
we have to give. Roots below:
a holy hunger fed by rain and sun.

Later, deer munch what growth remains after we've harvested
what you have provided, Lord of plenty.

Each begat is a new generation beholden to the former one.
The impulse for veneration competes with our own orbits.

Fishing nets sometimes yield surprises, like how you gather us,
O Lord, Unto you,
not rare pearls but similar expectant souls.

Vigil

Asleep in that hospital bed she looks already
dead, lids closed, breathing shallow, the hospital blanket
pulled over her useless breasts, the tray table watching over
her till her last end: small sponges on lollipop sticks
to moisten and apply like lipstick, a small rectangle
of tissues, a rosary that glows
in the dark, a paper menu never to be filled out,
a wrung-out, slightly damp washcloth.

Wilting flowers line the cold windowsill, greeting cards wait
to be shut and hauled home, a peace plant with one white bloom
lights the way, the IV drip of morphine hovering like an angel.

I was afraid the dusky light would crack the window.
She stirred and I held her hand like I was leading her
somewhere. Perhaps I was. I pulled up her blanket
like everyone does in these circumstances because
they don't know what else to do, because it somehow
makes the patient and the doer feel snugger.

When her eyes connected with mine I knew why I had lived.
I knew where I belonged. Nothing else mattered.
Nothing would stop the human race.

I spoke softly to her about family members
who would soon return to join this vigil,
idle talk about doctors and nurses
she could no longer recall, anything but more
silence, the thing there was most of.
She tried to squeeze my hand and I knew.

Black Box

I've always dreamt of California. Slipping the weather on and wearing it loosely. Driving Pacific Coast Highway too fast. Feeling the desert's dry heat baking my skin, the fog of San Francisco. I visited once, San Diego, and it was chilly and rainy the whole week. I never went back. I can always try Tahiti. If it comes to that. My sister wore a helmet with a face guard most of her adult life. When I took her places, people stared. I told myself I can kickbox them in the face. If it comes to that. Joni Mitchell said there are no victimless crimes I know of out here in these graffiti ruins, my love. She is right, of course. Who can I say this to? I can steal words from anyone. If it comes to that. Who listens to elders anymore/way? Who still says, my love? Lovers staring into the blue flames of a crackling fire? A horse whisperer to a thrashing mare? The sea and the moon in dialogue? I've always wanted to use the words cul-de-sac and cumulus together in a poem. I still can. If it comes to that. People used to be able to say what they felt. Now any word can be the wrong one in this new age of heresy and Puritans. I miss the light of Vermont, its green shine, walnut skulls, the anatomy of moonwort. In season, I take pansies to my sister's grave. I wait for someone to discover the black box that explains all this. Maybe it's best not knowing. If it comes to that.

All Evening the Luna Moths

—after a line by Mary Kay Rummel

ponder the inevitable—their short stay in the physical realm
each spring and early summer their large, translucent wings

seeing through—an auspice
their white bodies barely here
the moon moth few ever see
crescent in the eyespot of its wings

pinkish long legs, ghosts of a ballerina dancing
what will we say if we spot one by chance?

how can we not think of any life's purpose
what ties us to the physical world?

the luna moth lives for about a week
its leaving imminent
when adult, it no longer feeds as if the body is already spirit

the earth a sanctum where she lays her eggs
and dies, or does she?
eggs hatch into caterpillars

which body holds me to earth and for how long
the one you can barely see,
the one I insist on?

all evening the moths persist
an irony—eyespots and long tails on their hind legs

confuse predators as if their survival
is as important as ours

Incident on the Green Line

I am trying to quit thinking of simple human decency as a form of heroism, both in my poems and in the world.
—Gabrielle Calvocoressi

most sit on the el car
minding their own business
avoiding direct eye contact
strangers making love
to their phones or reading/
someone passes through
seeking change for food,
which many of us doubt,
but a few, the least among us,
comply, though most shake
their heads and look down
at anything/
there is the one talking loudly
to himself to invisible others
and we listen and are thankful/
a man just up and punches
an elderly woman in the face
and someone pushes the button for help
while others comfort her
a middle-aged woman lets the old woman
rest her head against her warm bosom
while others stare blankly or
shake their heads in commiseration
as two men stand in front of her
to block further attack
and I think how fast
ugliness appears and how fast
our better selves sing
yes, they sing

About the Author

Marc Frazier has published poetry in over one hundred literary journals online and in print including *Permafrost, Poet Lore, Evansville Review, The Spoon River Poetry Review, Another Chicago Magazine, The Gay and Lesbian Review,* and *Bloom.* He is the recipient of an Illinois Arts Council Award for poetry and has been featured on *Verse Daily.* He has been nominated for a Pushcart Prize and has received two Best of the Net nominations. Marc has published three full-length poetry books with Aldrich Press (Kelsay Books), Glass Lyre Press, and Adelaide Books in addition to two chapbooks. A sample of the anthologies he appears in include *New York Quarterly: Without a Doubt: Poems about Faith, New Poetry from the Midwest, Aeolian Harp Series: anthology of poetry folios* (Glass Lyre Press), and *Collateral Damage* (Glass Lyre Press). He has had residencies at Ragdale and Vermont Studio Center. He has also published book reviews, essays, flash fiction, and memoir excerpts in such venues as *Spillwords, Flash Fiction Magazine, South Shore Review, Cobalt,* and *Evening Street Review,* among others. He's done numerous poetry readings in the Chicago area and has led many poetry workshops over the years. Marc, now a Fort Lauderdale, LGBTQ writer, is active on social media, particularly on his Marc Frazier Author page on Facebook, mcfj24 on Instagram, and @marcfrazier45 on Twitter.